Pastoral

Burnout

And

Leadership

Styles

PASTORAL
BURNOUT
AND
LEADERSHIP
STYLES

**FACTORS CONTRIBUTING
TO STRESS AND MINISTERIAL TURNOVER**

RUBEN EXANTUS

authorHOUSE®

AuthorHouse™
1663 Liberty Drive
Bloomington, IN 47403
www.authorhouse.com
Phone: 1-800-839-8640

Published by AuthorHouse   12/04/2012

ISBN: 978-1-4772-9469-7 (sc)
ISBN: 978-1-4772-9468-0 (hc)
ISBN: 978-1-4772-9467-3 (e)

Library of Congress Control Number: 2012922407

Dedication

To my Lord Jesus Christ who receives all the glory, honor, praise, and credit for any positive results of this work. He is able to do immeasurably more than I ask or imagine, according to his power that is at work within me.

To my family: my wife Florence who, despite the tough times, has supported me through a sometimes difficult and seemingly endless journey; and to my children who had to deal with countless hours when I had to do this work.

To all of the pastors of Central Florida and around the world who faithfully serve God and His people despite the difficult challenges they face in church ministry.

Acknowledgements

This work is the result of many years of learning and development from people in my life including mentors, teachers, supporters, advisors, pastors, friends, and families, who invested time, energy and interest in me so that I can become what I am today. Words cannot express how grateful I am.

Nothing is achieved in life without the help of many people, known or unknown. Every successful person is the sum of what he or she has learned from others. Here are some of many who made this work possible:

To my wife Florence, for your unwavering support.

To my late parents Philomene J. and Paul C. Exantus.

To my sister Stael Exantus, who many years ago, supported me when I made my first step into the long journey of higher education.

To my longtime friend Nesthone Antoine, for your words of encouragement.

CONTENTS

Preface

Pastoral burnout and leadership styles is a concise paperback adapted from a research conducted on Southern Baptist pastors of Central Florida along with a compilation of teaching work at Rex Institute for Research and Leadership Development. Its streamlined approach will appeal to those pastors who want an authoritative account of pastoral leadership competencies. This book on pastoral burnout and leadership styles is dedicated to helping pastors, candidates for pastoral ministry, and individuals who want to have a better understanding of pastoral leadership.

The fundamental purpose of *Pastoral Burnout and Leadership Styles* is to assist pastors, candidates for pastoral ordination, and individual Christian leaders alike in furthering their abilities to lead others and get great things done for the Lord. Whether you're a volunteer, a part-time paid minister, or a pastor on the front line in full-time ministry, this book has been written to help you develop your capacity to guide others to reach new heights. This book revealed the factors that influence stress, burnout, and ministry turnover among Southern Baptist pastors in Central Florida. The central premise is that spiritual formation and Biblical training address the knowledge that pastors need to prevent pastoral burnout and ministry turnover. An important aspect of the book is to provide perceptions that stress, burnout, and lack of leadership development are perceived to be a path leading to ministry turnover. It appears that the majority of the seminaries do not provide adequate preparation for pastoral leadership development, and the Southern Baptist Convention does not provide sufficient training to pastors aiming at helping them to cope with ministry stress and burnout prevention.

This book is mostly about how Southern Baptist pastors exercise leadership. It reflects a study conducted in the Central Florida region, also known as Greater Orlando, which comprises counties that are often included in Central Florida demographics. It is primarily served by the Greater Orlando Baptist Association (GOBA), Ridge Baptist Association, Marion Baptist Association, Lake County Baptist Association, and Halifax Baptist Association. It comprises a rich, diverse multicultural population among the surrounding counties including European Americans, African Americans, Haitians, and Hispanics.

Introduction

This book is designed to create sustained conversations about pastoral burnout and leadership styles of pastors within the Southern Baptist Convention and other denominations across the United States and around the world. This conversation about pastoral burnout and leadership styles will help you understand the factors that cause burnout and shape leadership development for evangelical pastors in the United States.

Many people believe that being a pastor is among the world's most honorable professions. Pastoral ministry constitutes the highest privilege for those who profess the Christian faith. Nothing could be more honorable or have greater eternal significance than serving God in His church. However, fulfilling this privilege and discharging the pastoral responsibilities demands a lot of sacrifices and a thorough comprehension of the church and those who fill its pews. Furthermore, historically, persons who entered the ministry were most likely to spend the rest of their lives in it. Thus, leaving pastoral ministry was considered inconceivable to a faithful person. Today, however, it is not uncommon that a minister voluntarily leaves the church or otherwise is forced out by his own congregational body. Since the mid-1980s, the spiritual honeymoon between many pastors within the Southern Baptist convention and their congregation seems to last only a few years. Pastors seem to have more responsibilities today than in the past and that is taking a frightening toll on them. One reason may be that pastors are not equipped to deal with crisis management effectively.

Pastors today are faced with more work, more problems, and more stress than at any other time in the history of the church. According to a study conducted by Richard A. Murphy, 80 % of pastors feel unqualified and discouraged in their role, 80 % of seminary and Bible school graduates who enter the ministry will leave the ministry within the first five years, and 90 % of pastors said their seminary or Bible school training did only a fair to poor job preparing them for ministry. Church leadership comes with tremendous responsibilities that can overwhelm the clergy. Like any other model of leadership, church leadership is a complex phenomenon. While leadership in general has generated an extensive body of knowledge and theoretical models that focus on leaders' success, traits, styles and qualities; there is a lack of empirical research to demonstrate effectiveness of church leadership.

Although church leadership has been in the center of discussion among Christians since the beginning of Christianity, spiritual leadership is nonetheless a new era leadership model. Spiritual leadership is defined as a leadership model that supports others in connecting with their spiritual selves–which is the wellspring of creativity, values, and morality as well as finding one's calling in life. It is a new way of thinking that views the leader as a whole. It views the leader in his/her four dimensional being, which consists of the body, mind (logical/rational thought), heart (emotions, feelings), and spirit (means of communication with God). Pastors are spiritual leaders who must apply spiritual leadership principles such as providing time for clear self-awareness and reflection, encouraging wholeness mindsets to resolve issues, and building community and direction by discussing and aligning individual as well as group values.

Organizations, whether religious or secular, are complex systems. Organizational leaders need to acquire adequate leadership skills to effectively lead people and organizations. Leadership competencies including emotional intelligence skills are essential to pastoral ministry. However, leadership development is perhaps one of the weakest links in pastoral leadership and the lack of it can lead to ministry turnover. Leaders' overwhelming responsibilities, lack of organizational support and cooperation, as well as their personal factors tend to put them under high pressure and adversity. Such personal factors include the characteristics, strategies and behaviors that leaders employ within an event, intentionally or not, to navigate through and capture the learning. Shepherding a spiritual flock is not so simple; it comes with a price tag. So, true leadership, even when it is practiced by the most mature and emotionally stable person, always exacts a toll on him or her. Thus, pastors face great challenges as they lead their flock. Those who understand their divine calling should be aware of the immensity and weight of the pastoral task. As O.S. Hawkins stated, "there is high anxiety in the high calling of ministry. The pressures of the pastorate are especially intense breeding grounds for stress". With the tremendous responsibilities of leading God's flock comes the potential for either great blessings or great judgment. From a spiritual leadership point of view, good leaders are doubly blessed, and poor leaders are doubly chastened.

Furthermore, pastors like other leaders, face all kinds of battles in their daily lives including financial, spiritual, marital, vocational, and relational. The spiritual leader must apply the spiritual principles in order to win the battles of life. According to Rick Warren, "the spiritual leaders must identify their enemies, admit their own inadequacy, take their problems to the Lord, relax in faith, and thank Him in advance for the victory". Discouragement can be a factor in clergy abandonment. Studies show that there are at least four factors leading to discouragement. These factors include fatigue, frustration, failure, and fear. Many pastors get discouraged and abandon their ministry because of exhaustion. Fatigue is one of the main reasons for discouragement. Pastors who have worked themselves to exhaustion get discouraged and ultimately leave their post. They are worn out physically, mentally, and emotionally drained. Currently pastoral leadership is experiencing serious challenges. The church is succumbing to cultural and secular pressures. The way of religion in American culture has become the way of church and it is a wrong way. The church has conformed itself to the world. This is an evangelical disaster. It's the failure of the church to stand for truth as truth. Basically, the evangelical church has accommodated to the world spirit of the age. There is a prevailing confusion within the church body, which started during the early middle twentieth century. In 1956, Niebuhr lamented that the entire twentieth century has demonstrated the confusion that exists between the role of the church and the pastor. This confusing role creates a great deal of misunderstanding within the church body. Thus, pastoral leadership should be measured for authenticity. When authenticity is measured, many believe that a pastor's ministry can be perceived as more authentic. The argument of authenticity has been used in leadership studies as a measurement for spiritual leadership effectiveness. Authenticity implies that the leader acts in accord with the true self, expressing oneself in ways that are consistent with inner thoughts and feelings. A leader's awareness of his or her deeper self creates a greater spiritual and emotional intelligence and the willingness to communicate and behave from one's authentic self creates more valuable spiritual leadership.

Think of Pastoral Burnout and Leadership Styles as a guide to take along on your ministerial leadership journey. The first six chapters introduce you to pastoral burnout and the author's point of view about pastoral leadership. Chapter one through four describes pastoral burnout, pastoral ministry and leadership development. Chapter five describes the leadership competencies. In chapter six you will find a description of what we found regarding the factors leading to pastoral burnout and in chapter seven we talk about the action to take to avoid burnout. Each chapter is designed to help ministers understand the

challenge they face in ministry—the essential behaviors—
that pastors employ to get things done for the glory of the
Lord and to explain the fundamental leadership principles
that support their leadership practices. There is evidence
from our research and that of previous studies offered to
support the principles and we provide real examples of
real pastors who demonstrate the practice of a specific
leadership style and burnout behavior. There are also
specific recommendations on what you can do to avoid
your own burnout and to continue your development as a
leader.

Dr. W. Ruben Exantus

PART I

What Is Pastoral Burnout?

Chapter One

The Pastoral Ministry Challenges

P astoral leadership today faces unique challenges that create the need for leadership studies. A large number of pastors struggle to lead the flock. According to a research conducted by The Barna Group in 2006, pastors struggle with their interaction with others. The data in the study were based on a nationwide survey of 627 protestant senior pastors. The results revealed that many pastors struggle with personal relationships like other adults in the society. Being a spiritual leader of other people creates unusual relational dynamics and expectations. One of those areas is often a lost sense of connection with others; 61 % of pastors surveyed admitted that they have few close friends; 1 in every 6 of them feels underappreciated. Pastors also deal with family problems. According to the results, 1 in every 5 contends that they are currently dealing with a very difficult family situation. The morale within the pastoral ministry environment seems to be declining.

Apparently, this decline is due to job dissatisfaction, frustration, stress, and lack of supply and support. Some scholars such as Caroll and Niebuhr even view ministry as a troubled profession. The Barna Group went so far as to say that clergy is one of the most frustrated occupational groups in the United States. Sadly, a great number of pastors would be seen as second-rate practitioners had they ended up in any other field. According to a study conducted by Klaas and Klaas in 1999, 30 % of the clergy interviewed expressed satisfaction with their work; another 30 % expressed moderate degrees of satisfaction; and half of the remaining 40 % were in what they called advanced stages of burnout. The typical comments noted include "the joy is gone; I can't take the crap anymore, or I cannot encourage others into this or young people see this and say, no way". So, the pastors are discouraged, dissatisfied and willing to quit.

Furthermore, many who are engaged in the ministry seem to lack adequate theological education and leadership development skills that allow them to attain success. The expectations for clergy are higher than ever before. There are high expectations for graduates of higher education institutions. Not all schools and seminaries who train leaders for the ministry produce the type of graduates that possess the knowledge, skills, and values in the real world. Many of the American seminaries are failing to train leaders for the twenty-first century. Leaders who have developed soft leadership skills such as visioning, motivation, and communication appear to be more successful than those who have not. Many scholars believed that the leadership behaviors that truly make a difference in organizational leaders can be developed. A leadership crisis seems prevalent in America's evangelical church. The church is more demanding today than it was fifty years ago. The culture that its leaders have to deal with has changed. Therefore the church leaders must be equipped to deal with the challenges of the new area.

According to researchers, the average pastor today does not think of himself as a natural leader. He feels ill equipped for the leadership demands. Nonetheless, the average church attendee expects more than ever from his pastor. Previous studies conducted on forced terminations in the Southern Baptist Convention revealed that 1056 pastors were being terminated annually in the 1980s. In fact, 72,000 pastors were fired across America in 1999, and 50 % of pastors who work full time quit in five years. In response to concerns like these, a study of the quality of the church leadership and the factors that lead to pastors' burnout and turnover revealed necessary. This will create sustained conversation about pastoral leadership within the Southern Baptist denomination, the changes impacting it, and ways of strengthening it.

Pastoral ministry, in many denominations, commences with high ideals and great expectations. However, after a few years in service, the ministry can become a source of stress, which causes low self-confidence and a sense of powerlessness in the lives of many ministers. The problem is that there is burnout due to lack of information about the very factors that cause pastoral stress, ministerial turnover, and how the lack of leadership skills may be related to pastoral burnout in the Southern Baptist organization. Thus, I explored these factors to find out whether clergy leadership development helps pastors cope with the challenges inherent to their functions. It was an examination of the clerical functions, leadership development, and their interaction with the members of their congregation. This also identified the factors that influence clergy burnout, which eventually leads to a significant ministry turnover rate.

The rationale behind this work is the merger of two important topics: leadership development and burnout prevention. First, while leadership is being studied extensively for business leaders, many researchers have concluded that there is still a lack of empirical studies on leadership development of pastors. Second, the area of pastoral ministry has recently been experiencing a significant number of ministers' burnout and turnovers. Many concerns have been raised as to the potential leadership effectiveness of ministers. So far, there is no statistical information available concerning ministers' actual leadership behavior.

While many studies have been conducted to understand the dynamics of burnout in business, few studies have focused on the effect of burnout on the clergy. Some researchers have produced great results, which give interesting insights relating to the effect of burnout on the professional populations, such as teachers, psychiatric doctors, and school psychologists. Understanding factors leading to pastoral burnout could be an invaluable help to pastors for the maintenance of their own well-being as they help their followers. Pastoral tenure among the Southern Baptist Convention, the largest Protestant denomination in the United States, is three to four years.

The factors that contribute to pastors' burnout within the Southern Baptist Convention were examined through a presumed cause and effect concept.

Presumed Cause and Effect of Burnout

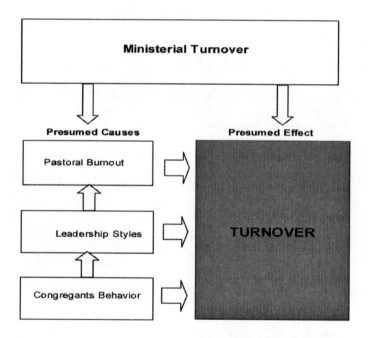

This was a significant study, which provided pastors with information in a real life setting that presents evidence of pastors' stress, burnout, leadership experience, and a ministry turnover rate within the Southern Baptist Convention. It also provided pastors with the evidence of the perceived cause and effect of pastoral burnout and helped SBC pastors to discover the sources of their own stress and burnout, which should eventually reduce the organization's turnover.

Furthermore, this study laid a foundation for further work that could show the reasons causing clergy burnout in other denominations. Knowing the factors influencing pastoral burnout could significantly reduce the turnover rate in pastoral ministry. By knowing the factors, pastors in the ministry and those that are preparing to enter the ministry would be prepared better to face the challenges that the profession entails. The potential benefits include the enhancements of knowledge within the Southern Baptist organization as well as the participants in the study, which include the pastors, other leaders, and the religious community; it would also help seminaries to better prepare pastors for the ministry. This will also help further research for organizational growth and pastoral leadership development.

Pastoral Burnout

Burnout Defined

Christina Maslach, a leading expert in the measure of burnout, defined burnout as a prolonged response to chronic work-related stress. It is a condition in which the person is not just tired, stressed, or disillusioned, but rather is in a zone of pain. Earlier studies conducted on burnout support the notion that it is a response to work overload. Burnout and feelings of exhaustion are common problems workers of all fields experience in the modern-day workplace, which eventually lead to other work-related problems such as sick leaves, absenteeism, turnovers, and mental health. Work overload, emotional exhaustion, depersonalization, and reduced professional efficacy are among the psychological factors that can cause one to experience burnout. Previous research has been conducted to deal with the problem of burnout. Primarily, the focus of the research has been on training individuals to change their work-related behaviors as well as some organizational approaches.

In 1984, Jayaratne and Chess studied burnout among social workers, mental health, and family services workers. They found that the determining factors of burnout were different in each field studied. Factors such as depersonalization, role ambiguity, role conflict, and stress were higher in social workers than mental health or family services workers. Several factors contribute to "burnout" among people who work in health and human services. According to Maslach, these factors include (a) working with families in crisis, (b) receiving little positive feedback or support, (c) having an outward focus, (d) lack of power or control to change problems combined with the influence of funding source requirements, (e) difficulty in defining role as a result of the conflict between the implicit and explicit rules governing the client relationship, (f) experience in the field of social work is a fairly narrow focus which creates difficulty in changing careers, (g) demanding workload, (h) low social support, and (i) feeling ineffectual. Studies conducted by many researchers have also shown that job dissatisfaction is a contributing factor to burnout.

The question whether one is burned out is not always noticed by the person when it happens. The individuals experiencing burnout are often unable to see any hope of positive change in their situations. Burnout is often caused by excessive and prolonged stress. Being in a state of emotional, mental, and physical exhaustion, the burnout person feels overwhelmed and unable to meet the situational challenges they face. The most significant developmental experiences tend to be the ones that put leaders under high pressure and adversity. Personal factors are also critical in capturing the lessons of experience. Personal factors include the characteristics, strategies, and behaviors that leaders employ within the event, intentionally or not, to navigate through and capture the learning.

Additionally, a leader's learning agility is a great personal asset. Lombardo and Eichinger identified four dimensions that comprise the personal aspects of a leader's learning agility; that is, the ability of the leader to learn as they go. The four dimensions include: [a] People agility, which means self-awareness, treating others well, and resilience under pressure. [b] Results agility, meaning getting results in tough conditions, inspiring others, and having self-confidence. [c] Mental agility, which means problem-solving ability, comfort with ambiguity. [d] Change agility, which means curiosity, openness to experimentation.

Because effective leadership is crucial to a church organization's ability to succeed, it is imperative for pastors to avoid the crippling effects of burnout.

Pastoral Burnout Defined

When we studied burnout among SBC pastors, the purpose was to find the factors that influence pastoral burnout and describe the connection between clergy stress, burnout, ministry turnover, and leadership development. The terms stress and burnout were used as they are uniformly described and defined by the many scholars and clergy who have studied the subject. The term "leadership", as defined by leadership expert P.G. Northouse, was used as "a process whereby an individual influences a group of individuals to achieve a common goal". Burnout is found most often among those who work in human services or among those who bear heavy responsibilities, therefore, often among pastors.

The causes for burnout are usually role overload or role confusion and inability of a person to share responsibilities and to take time off work. Many Christian researchers who work in the field of psychology, theology, and Christian counseling believe that burnout can be headed off or overcome by prayer, Scripture reading, physical therapy and exercise, spiritual development, free time and having a support system. According to Charles L. Rassieur, the issue for the church as it copes with pastoral burnout is how to keep it at a manageable level so that the pastor does not conclude that the only viable option is to leave the ministry. If this is a correct assumption, it is important that a burnout study takes into consideration the role that the congregants play, the minister's reaction to stress, his spiritual formation, and his leadership development as he performs his ministerial tasks.

Today's pastors face numerous demands from the ministry. A classic research study on pastors conducted by Fuller Institute of Church Growth in 1991 revealed some startling statistics that have continued to trend and still carry weight in the 21st century. According to the survey, 93 % of pastors work more than 46 hours a week, and 80 % believed pastoral ministry affected their families negatively. Furthermore, 33 % believed ministry was a hazard to their family, 70 % reported a significant stress related crisis at least once in their ministry, and nearly 50 % of ministers felt unable to meet the needs of the job, while 90 % felt inadequately trained to cope with ministry demands.

In addition, a larger percentage of ministers, about 70 % say they have lower self-esteem now compared to when they started in ministry, 40 % reported a serious conflict with a parishioner at least once a month, and 70 % do not have someone they consider a close friend. In 2003, O.S.

Hawkins found out that "the top 2 prescriptions prescribed to Southern Baptist ministers in 2002 were both related to stress problems".

Steve Bagi, after twenty-one years in pastoral ministry, contended that "the church is losing good leaders through burnout and disillusionment; and whatever the rate is, it is too high". Pastoral burnout is a major ministry problem. But fortunately, it is a preventable illness.

Burnout: A Preventable Mental Illness

Burnout is a mental illness frequently diagnosed among care-giving professionals including psychologists, social workers, and leaders in the ministry. Its symptoms include fatigue, tension and exhaustion, anxiety, worry, insecurity and even guilt. It is, however, a malady that can be prevented. According to J.S. Haskell, there are four factors that tend to promote prevention of burnout: (a) self-awareness—those who seek to provide care must be aware of their own personal strengths, values, weaknesses and blind spots as they seek to help others identify their own; (b) balance—maintaining balance involves setting limits and boundaries around oneself emotionally, spiritually, psychologically and even physically if needed. It also includes working in an environment in which expectations are clearly communicated and set. The clergy need help and cannot do this alone. They need assistance from their congregants to help them with the establishment of boundaries; (c) social connectedness—they need to experience the social support that comes through intimate and authentic relationships among equals. Clergy need to be able to be open about their struggles and be challenged, encouraged, receive support and be held accountable; (d) continued education—these opportunities serve to broaden their horizons, develop extended social networks, stimulate and energize them for the work they do and allow them to step out beyond their local ministries.

The pastoral ministry is classified among helping professionals that are especially prone to burnout. The issues that pastors face are usually those leading to burnout in other helping professions. Such issues include inordinate time demands, unrealistic expectations, isolation, and loneliness. This results in the pastors' personal lives being severely imbalanced, and their spiritual lives ironically dry.

Pastoral burnout may result in a loss of interest and passion for the work of ministry to which the pastor was called as well as physical and marital problems. In 2009, Jin conducted a study on 68 Korean-American Presbyterian pastors. According to the results, the top ten factors which have threatened ministry were extreme fatigue, stagnation, lack of intellectual ability, loss of ministry vision, excessive work, economic difficulty, increasing worry and impatience, conflict, comparison with colleagues, and loss of passion.

Furthermore, Jin noted that "burnout brings about not only the loss of passion for ministry or abandonment of ministry, but also physical and emotional sickness, and trouble and conflict between husband and wife". Based on previous studies, it is an undeniable fact that pastors are at risk for burnout. But, today not enough research exists on burnout and its impact on the functions of the pastor. There have been studies that explored the risk factors of burnout and its effects on marriage, clergy loneliness, and family adjustment, but only a handful have focused on the factors that contribute to pastoral burnout. There have been studies on burnout prevention and mitigation, but most of them have been on individual coping. Few studies have explored the effects of leadership development theories on pastoral burnout. Therefore, it is safe to say that less research has been devoted to understanding leadership development as it relates to pastoral burnout. A careful empirical study is necessary to gain a complete understanding of the impact of burnout factors on the clergy to reduce pastoral burnout. The understanding of leadership development theories such as spiritual formation, servant leadership, transformational leadership, leader-member exchange, and the skills of emotional intelligence is vital to pastoral ministry.

Chapter Two

Foundations of Pastoral Leadership

A church is a transformational agent in every city or town. It plays a transformational role in peoples' lives. Strong communities are built around churches. Healthy local churches led by capable, honest, and committed pastors transform the moral fabric of communities in a unique and positive way: the way of God. Pastoral ministry is an essential calling. The calling of a pastor is a noble work, which demands the greatest respect and the greatest leadership. According to the Apostle Paul's instruction to Timothy in 1Timothy 3:1, "This is a true saying: if a man desires the office of an overseer, he desires a noble work". The office of pastoral leadership, if rightly understood, is the most honorable and important position that a person in the world can ever hold. It's the greatest employment on earth with an eternal value and significance. Every day, as I seek to know Him better, I wonder the reasons why God in His infinite wisdom would assign this office to guilty and imperfect human beings.

The foundation of pastoral leadership is deeply rooted in the pastor's calling. It's a threefold calling. The first part of a pastor's call is to salvation. You can't shepherd God's people if you don't know Him. The call to salvation precedes any calling to pastoral ministry. The second call is to service. Pastoral leadership is all about service. We can't ascend to the role of overseer without learning how to serve first. As Christians, serving means living as Jesus lived. Jesus is our example. When we pattern our lives after Jesus we will serve God as He did. Jesus said to His disciples, "You know that the rulers of the Gentiles lord it over them, and those who are great exercise authority over them. Yet it shall not be so among you; but whoever desires to become great among you, let him be your servant. And whoever desires to be first among you, let him be your slave— just as the Son of Man did not come to be served, but to serve, and to give His life a ransom for many" (Matthew 20:25-28, New King James Bible, 1982).

So, the key to becoming an overseer and great leader is to be a servant of others, just as Jesus came to serve others and not to be served. Now this runs contrary to the "me-first" mentality or the quick-fix pastors of our days.

Jesus is saying that you become great by serving God and others rather than serving yourself. Many of us are self-serving rather serving others. Learning to serve is foundational to pastoral leadership.

The third and final step is the calling to full-time ministry. The call to pastoral ministry has to be confirmed before one puts himself upon a church to pastor. Occasionally, a prophetic voice may rise up to confirm a call, which may not be recognized by others in the church as a prophetic voice. But, most of the time, the church confirms the gifts that God has given to the ones He calls to pastoral ministry. So the third thing is confirmation.

Furthermore, those who desire this noble work have to be trained. This includes training in pastoral character, laying a foundation of biblical knowledge, and pastoral leadership skills. Leading God's flock with conviction and competence, teaching with authority, and preaching God's word with passion are skills set a pastor needs to learn. When a pastor has these skills under his belt, he is a competent leader ready to lead the flock of God.

Pastoral Integrity

A trustworthy leader will increase tenure and make his organization more effective. The practice of good leadership principles enable leaders to work well with followers and peers. Servant leadership is an attitude with which the leader should approach the leadership task. It is not bound by the situation. It rather exercised more or less easily depending on the context. Leadership integrity is the driving force behind a person of influence.

Many people who go to church today are viewed as religious individuals rather Christians. They are called churchgoers and do not trust their leaders because of ethical issues. Without trust, managing people the right way can be very difficult.

Many have become leaders because of some natural ability instilled in them at conception. Other leaders acquired their position by inheritance, seniority, training and so forth. The position they now hold, may come with great responsibility for the people in their organization. However, ethical issues are rampant within the Christian community. Who can you trust and why? What are the characteristics of an ethical leader? Do religious followers really care about ethical issues? These are questions many people ask when it comes to pastoral leadership.

In every religious organization, there is a code of conduct that dictates the way of living of its followers. The Koran determines the way of living for the Muslims, the Vedas are the common Holy scripture for the Hindus, and so forth. The Bible is the basis for determining a Christian way of life. A Christian must walk with the ethical conduct taught in scripture. The Christian who desires a leadership position, in addition to being a person of influence, must be a person of character and integrity. In other words, he or she must be honest. Honesty is not just the best policy for the Christian, it is the only policy. There are no other options for him or her. Unfortunately, this is not always the case. According to P.G. Northouse, one of the leadership traits that are so crucial to great leadership is integrity. Integrity is the quality of honesty and trustworthiness.

It is commonly agreed among Christians that Jesus Christ is the head of the church. He then delegates His authority to be exercised through the government of the church. However, the method of government of the church is sometimes an object of debate, and is considered as one of the primary differences between some denominations. The Bible provides the ground for church government through the authority of its offices, but is silent in the specific methods of implementation. Generally speaking, churches in America and around the world function within three prominent leadership styles. First, there is the Episcopal style, which is a system of church of government in which the bishop is the principal leader.

In this system, decisions are made at levels higher than the local church. Second, there is the Presbyterian style, a system of church government that acknowledges Christ as the head alone and rules the church spiritually by the Bible. The leaders then have ministerial and declarative authority, but not legislative. Third, the congregational style, an autonomous form of church government which allows a local church the freedom to determine what the will of God is. It's a democratic leadership philosophy.

This type of leadership style, however, creates tension to authority relationships in the church. It is the tension between the authority of the principal leaders and the authority of the congregation.

Whatever leadership style that is adopted, the pastor is a standout individual and is seen all the time. Pastors are models to their followers. To exercise good spiritual leadership authority, a pastor has to possess a great deal of character in order to influence followers. Character inspires people's confidence. If you are a pastor, you should outpace the rest of your team, above all, in character and integrity. And this should be observed by both your leadership team and the congregation as a whole.

Many Christian leaders don't understand their role as community leaders when it comes to ethical issues. Some years ago, my wife was invited speak on health and family counseling at a radio station in our community. After the program, she received a phone call from someone who claimed to be a minister going through some tough times. He also expressed that he had a lot of family issues. He asked her if she could lend him some money. How strange! The minister kept calling and my wife who is a person with a good heart, in an effort to help said, call my husband perhaps our church could help you. The man never called the church nor did he call the pastor. But, he kept on sending us text messages. One day I replied to him and felt the urge to write a few sentences about Christian ethics. He replied and said, "I have my master's in theology and I don't see the word ethics in the Bible". This is really sad.

There are several distinguishing characteristics of Christian ethics. Christians believe that their ethics is based on God's will and His revelation. Therefore it is absolute and prescriptive. The genuine Christian leader is a person of integrity whose ethics is rooted on the moral attributes of God. The most important characteristic for a leader in 21st century will be trust. Because of numerous scandals at the end of the last millennium and in the beginning of this new century, followers in the workplace and churches have become somewhat skeptical about their leaders' motives. This is true in both secular and religious world. Leaders must build trust, create a sense of meaning and purpose, and establish a meaningful dialogue with their followers. The leaders of the 21st century will have to demonstrate some level of leadership integrity. They must lead by example. Creating visions and setting goals may not be good enough. The leaders must demonstrate that there is meaning behind these visions and goals. Leadership is all about the example we set, not the position we hold. A river never rises above its source. As leaders lead, they must be open to dialogue and initiate the process. This will certainly win the commitment of the followers who will have great confidence in their leader. The 21st century leader must be trustworthy in order to influence followers and instill confidence in them, which will make them feel strong, qualified, and ready to successfully achieve the goals and objectives of their organization.

Chapter Three

Pastoral Ministry and Leadership Development

Pastoral Ministry

Pastoral ministry is sometimes misunderstood. Often, men enter into the ministry and don't quite understand what it entails. The main purpose of pastoral ministry is the guarding of souls. Basically, it's the imagery contained in the word overseer. Everything else the pastor does come from this idea which means all his tasks are controlled by it. The overseer is one called by God and set aside by the church to watch over the souls that the Lord puts under his care. As part of this ministry of guarding souls, pastors are also involved in peoples' lives, leading and bringing more souls to God.

The apostle Peter expressed some key principles of pastoral ministry when he wrote:

> The elders who are among you I exhort, I who am a fellow elder and a witness of the sufferings of Christ, and also a partaker of the glory that will be revealed: Shepherd the flock of God which is among you, serving as overseers, not by compulsion but willingly, not for dishonest gain but eagerly; nor as being lords over those entrusted to you, but being examples to the flock (1 Peter 5:1-3, New King James Bible, 1982).

The ministry of the pastor is to shepherd the flock of God. A shepherd is a person who cares for a flock of sheep. He has the responsibility to feed and lead them safely. While leading, the shepherd keeps the flock together, so it is safe from attack. The sheep may be many, but each sheep receives individual attention. Those that go astray are brought back to the flock, and if one is sick the shepherd provides treatment making sure that the sheep is healed. Nonetheless, each one is known by name.

In pastoral ministry, every Christian receives individual care. It is the responsibility of the pastor to make sure that each is helped to grow to full Christian maturity according to the measure of God's grace.

Pastors do this by teaching the Word of God faithfully, nurturing, and binding up the broken-hearted. The pastor must also discipline those that wander the way of God. As Paul told Titus, "Speak these things, exhort, and rebuke with all authority" (Titus 2:15, New King James Bible, 1982). This is the ministry of the pastor-teacher. The pastor, however, must understand the Biblical principle of authority. Pastors should not dominate the lives of those put under his care. Some pastors abuse their pastoral authority. In the flock, there are always young sheep. Young sheep are dependent on the shepherd to survive in dangerous situations. So, it is very easy for young Christians to become too dependent on their pastors. It is the responsibility of the pastor to teach the Christians to read their Bible, listen to the voice of God, and follow the leading of the Spirit so they can grow on their own. The apostle John encourages Christians to allow the Holy Spirit to lead them and keep them faithful to what they had been taught from the beginning. He wrote:

> But the anointing which you have received from Him abides in you, and you do not need that anyone teach you; but as the same

anointing teaches you concerning all things, and is true, and is not a lie, and just as it has taught you, you will abide in Him (1 John 2:27, New King James Bible, 1982).

This is an excellent example of what the teaching role of the pastor is in the church. There will always be agents of Satan who come to teach false doctrine to the flock. When it happens, it is the responsibility of the pastor to lead them the proper way. When false doctrine threatened members of the true body of believers, the apostle John found it necessary to spell out to them the dangers in it, even though the brethren had been thoroughly grounded in the truth. Pastors need to reassure their members that their foundational beliefs were true when they accepted the Lord. Whenever necessary, they need to explain the truth to them again. They also need to encourage the Christians to trust the Holy Spirit to lead them into the truth.

Leadership Development of Pastors

There have been numerous studies conducted in leadership in general, but little research exists on leadership development in pastoral ministry. Leadership competencies are important to pastoral ministry. To date, most of the research conducted on pastoral leadership has been focused on impairment, burnout, and misconduct. The role of followers and their relationship with their leaders in pastoral ministry has not been defined, which sometimes creates confusion. The role that followers play can affect a leader's behavior and effectiveness of a church. The leader-member relationship is a process that is centered on the interactions between leaders and followers. Leadership functions better when the process is well understood by both leader and follower.

Pastors often face identity crises as the church succumbs to cultural and secular pressures as well as religious unrest. Pastoral theology is for the most part a field without a clear definition. Its precise meaning and component parts seem to vary widely from one denomination to the next and from one seminary to the next. According to some researchers adequate ministerial training goes far beyond Biblical training. They suggested that ministerial training should incorporate sufficient leadership development training including emotional intelligence competencies, mobilizing for innovation and change, applied problem solving, vision casting, teamwork, and time management. Perhaps the pastors' and congregants' role in the church should be redefined. According to John McArthur, "redefining the church leads inevitably to redefining the pastoral role", which he added, spills over into pastoral role training at the seminary level. Many believe that American seminaries that prepare leaders for pastoral ministry have done a less than adequate job. In fact, Aubrey Malphurs in a research published in 2003 stated that a leadership crisis exists in the evangelical church in America. The modern theological schools and seminaries fail to train leaders for the 21st century.

Statistics show that the top ten (10) largest seminaries in North America for the past five years have been evangelical and five of them are Southern Baptist Seminaries. By order of number of enrolled students, they are: Fuller Theological Seminary (Inter), Southwestern Baptist Theological Seminary (SBC), Southeastern Baptist Theological Seminary (SBC), Southern Baptist Theological Seminary (SBC), Dallas Theological Seminary (Inter), Gordon-Conwell Theological Seminary (Inter), Trinity Evangelical Divinity School (EFCA), Asbury Theological Seminary (Inter), Golden Gate Baptist

Theological Seminary (SBC), and New Orleans Baptist Theological Seminary (SBC).

The Southern Baptist Convention (SBC) is the largest Protestant denomination in America with 16,136,044. According to Hartford Institute for religious research, SBC ranked #2 in 2011, down 0.15 percent from the year previous year. The Association of Theological Schools reported 251 member schools in the United States and Canada in 2005. Of those schools, 141 were Protestant, 53 were non-denominational or inter-denominational, 54 were Roman Catholic, and three were Orthodox Christian.

Top 10 Largest Seminaries in America (2009-2010)					
Rank	Name	Enrollment	Denomination	State	Leadership Program
1	Fuller Theological Seminary	1940	Inter	CA	LDP
2	SouthWestern Baptist Theological Sem.	1477	SBC	TX	NLDP
3	SouthEastern Baptist Theological Sem.	1430	SBC	NC	NLDP
4	Southern Baptist Theological Sem.	1364	SBC	KY	LDP
5	Dallas Theological Seminary	1108	Inter	TX	LDP
6	Gordon-Conwell Theological Sem.	1037	Inter	MA	PLDP
7	Trinity Evangelical Divinity School	908	EFCA	IL	NLDP
8	Asbury Theological Seminary	781	Inter	KY	NLDP
9	Golden Gate Baptist Theological Sem.	772	SBC	CA	NLDP
10	New Orleans Baptist Theological Sem.	656	SBC	LA	NLDP

FLDP = Full Leadership Program

NLDP = No Leadership Program

LDMP = Leadership ministry programs such as black church leadership, women's leadership, worship leadership, etc.

PLDP = Partial leadership programs--none in M.Div. Curriculum

SBC = Southern Baptist Convention

Inter = Interdenominational

EFCA = Evangelical Free Church of America

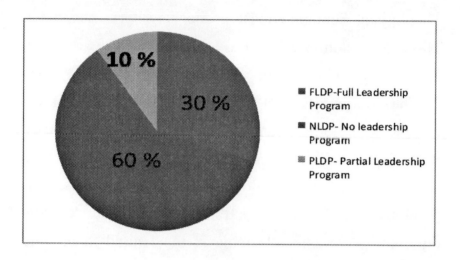

Top Ten Seminaries in US and Canada
Leadership Training Chart

Leadership Defined

Leadership is one the most misunderstood terms in organizational circles including churches, ministries, management, and government. Because it is misunderstood, therefore, it is misapplied. P.G. Northouse defined the term leadership as "a process whereby an individual influences a group of individuals who come together to achieve a common goal". Leadership involves influence; it is learned behavior and is concerned with how leaders affect followers. A learned behavior is a behavior that was observed by an individual that they find it to be beneficial to them in some way. There's a motivating factor behind any learned behavior. The learned behavior is a conditioned response to a stimuli through either voluntary or involuntary intent. It is some type of action or reflex that you learn. For example tying your shoes is a learned behavior, but crying is not. A learned behavior is a behavior that you decide to learn, unlike "innate" behavior. This is not a natural behavior. Instead it is learned by the person who decides to learn it. You can learn a behavior by watching others do it. For instance, riding a bike or learning to write. But Influence is the *sine qua non* of leadership. Without influence leadership does not exist.

Leadership occurs in groups. Groups are the context in which leadership takes place. It involves influencing a group of individuals who have a common purpose. In other words, as John Maxwell stipulates, "a leader is a person of influence or influencer who has integrity with people and impacts their lives greatly". Such person, Maxwell added, nurtures people, has faith in them, listens and leads people with care, understands people, enlarges people, navigates for people, connects with people, empowers people, and reproduces other influencers.

Leadership is a relationship between the leader and the follower. If no one is following, then no one is leading. We may be doing some wonderful, creative, and provocative things but, that in itself is not leadership. If two or more people come together and no one steps into leadership, we are a collective perhaps with a good idea, a vision, or an agenda but without a process for moving forward there is no leadership. Leadership happens in the relationship whether it is between two people, a team, a whole organization, a church, or a community. As in any relationship, a leadership relationship is characterized by attributes such as assumptions, expectations, values, emotions, successes, failures, dreams, and disappointments.

Leadership versus Management

Leadership and management are related, but different. However, they are similar in many ways. Both involve influence and working with people. They're both concerned with goal accomplishment. However, there is a big difference in how they operate. The primary functions of a management are planning, organizing, staffing, and controlling. He or she pays attention to details. The primary functions of leadership are to produce change, movement, and activities to reach goals and objectives. While different in capacity, leadership and management both complement each other. To be effective, an organization needs to have both competent management and leadership.

Leader versus Manager

Manager Produces order and consistency	Leader Produces change and movement
Planning / Budgeting Establishes agenda Set time tables Allocates resources	*Establishing Direction* Creates a vision Clarifies big picture Set strategies
Organizing / Staffing Provides structure Makes job placements Establishes rules and procedures	*Aligning People* Communicates goals Seeks Commitment Builds teams and coalitions
Controlling / Problem Solving Develops Incentives Generates Creative Solutions Takes Corrective Actions	*Motivating and Inspiring* Inspires and energizes Empowers subordinates Satisfies unmet needs

Effective Leadership

Becoming an effective leader takes time. All successful investors know it takes a long time to make good money doing investments. To be successful in investments requires time, patience, and resilience. Your success depends on what you do day after day over a long period of time. Leadership is the same way. Successful leaders invest in their leadership development. When leaders invest in their leadership development, the final result is leadership growth over time.

Some say that leaders are born. But, this is not entirely true. Leaders aren't born; they are made. Some may have been born with some leadership traits instilled in them at conception, but they need to be developed. The process of leadership is long, complicated and has made elements. Respect, dignity, discipline, people skills, vision, emotional intelligence, opportunity, preparedness and experience are just some of the intangible elements which come into play when talking leadership. Whether they were born with special gifts or not, all leaders can increase their leadership potential over a period of time if they can understand the leadership process.

John Maxwell argued that there are five levels of leadership and conceived of each level as a practice that could be used to lead more effectively. These levels of leadership he called principles include: 1) Leadership from Position—the lowest level of leadership. People follow you because they have to. Your ability to lead people is totally geared to your position and does not exceed beyond the lines of your job description or the authority granted to you by the company and your boss. 2) Leadership from Permission—a leadership based entirely on relationship. People follow you because they want to, not because you are in a position. The core of leadership of this level is that people who work with you want to know that you care about them, before they care about what you know. 3) Leadership from Production—a leadership based on results. People follow you because of what you have done for the organization, church, or the company. 4) Leadership from People Development—a leadership level whereby leaders use their position, relationships, and productivity to invest in their followers and develop them until these followers become leaders. People follow them because of what they have done for them personally. 5) Pinnacle—this is the highest level of leadership. People follow leaders at this level because of who they are and what they represent. According to Maxwell, only naturally gifted leaders ever make it to this highest level of leadership (about 5% of all leaders).

Every leader should aspire to grow beyond leadership level 1 to be effective. Effective leadership requires trust, which will produce long lasting professional relationships; the leader needs to be prepared to initiate and accept responsibility for growth by developing a purpose and seeing it through to completion; the leader needs to place a priority on developing people; and strive to leave an indelible mark on the organization and the people. The Bible called pastors to at least reach level four leadership development. Paul encouraged Timothy to develop leaders when he wrote, "And the things that you have heard from me among many witnesses, commit these to faithful men who will be able to teach others also" (2 Timothy: 2:2, New King James Bible, 1982).

The Pastor's Role

Traditionally, a pastor is believed to be a person called by God to provide spiritual direction and pursue a vision for His flock, the church. According to the Bible the church is called the flock of God and God's heritage (1 Peter 5:2 & 3, New King James Bible, 1982). Thus, the pastor's duty is to feed the flock with God's Word and to lead them in the proper way. Therefore, the church leader, the pastor is a direct link to God and God's wishes. When a pastor does not fulfill this role the congregation, inevitably, has a feeling of abandonment.

Some believe that pastors play various roles in the church. According to Muller, "pastors should be included in the category of human services workers because of the various roles and activities that make up a pastor's job, such as the roles of a counselor, teacher, preacher, and manager". Thus, the work of a pastor in the church is varied both in kind and scope. The three highest contributors to stress for a pastor are role ambiguity, role conflict, and role overload. According to Oswald Sanders, role ambiguity occurs when a pastor does not have within himself a road map guiding him as to what it means to be a resident religious authority. The more ambiguous the role the higher the stress level that is involved. Role conflict occurs when two or more people or groups have conflicting expectations for the pastor. Role overload has its source in role conflict, because after hearing each person's expectations, the pastor discovers how impossible it is to fulfill everyone's expectations. Overload is the pressure to do more work, not completing the day's work, and the amount of work that interferes with what has to be done. If the work's nature is more intangible and qualitative, overload is especially burdensome.

Burnout is identified as a major component of the ministerial retention problems. Previous studies showed that there is a shortage of pastors in the American churches. In a study conducted by Klaas and Klaas in 1999, they found that clergy retention was adversely impacted by burnout and mismatch between clergy and congregation. They also reported a lack of support for clergy family, low compensation, and internal conflicts as factors for ministerial shortage. The study reported that 20 % of clergy were experiencing burnout while another 20 % were on their way. So, we can understand why the Southern Baptist organization and other dominations across the

United States have so many churches without a shepherd. This leads to growing demands for pastors in the United States. Many pastors appear to be losing their motivation to serve. Despite a growing demand for ministers, studies show that an unusually large numbers of pastors are leaving the ministry. In 2008, C.L. Baucum studied the relationship between motivation and engagement in leaders. The population of leaders used in the study was Baptist pastors. The sample comprised 591 ministers in all three Texas Baptist Associations. The research found that there was a significant correlation between motivation and engagement in leaders. Also, the research uncovered variables that affected the correlation between ministers' motivation and engagement: "(a) the relative harmony/ conflict within the church, (b) the minister's relationship with the lay leaders of the church, (c) perception of stress in the home of the minister, and (d) whether the minister would continue to pastor if he had independent financial security".

Seminaries play a crucial role in preparing pastors for the ministry. The church needs capable leaders who are experts in Scripture as well as in leadership competencies— persons who can wisely apply their theological training to real life circumstances. Higher education has dramatically changed over the last 25 years, primarily because of the rise of non-traditional students in colleges, universities, and seminaries. The United States Department of Education defined a non-traditional higher education student as a student who has one of the following characteristics: delays enrollment, attends part-time for at least part of the academic year, works full-time while enrolled, is considered financially independent for purposes of determining eligibility for financial aid, has dependents other than a spouse, is a single parent, or does not have a high school diploma. According to some researchers, a larger number of non-traditional students have populated higher education campuses in America over the past 25 years. These non-traditional student trends are found in both secular and theological American education. Studies have shown that the typical seminary student of the 21st century is very different from the seminary student of a generation ago. Students entering seminary are older and more experienced in other careers than previous generations.

Due to this shift in higher education, seminaries have diversified to meet the need by offering one path instead of losing potential ministerial candidates. The expectations are higher for seminary graduates in the 21st century than generations ago. So, many question whether these seminaries are producing the type of graduates that possess the knowledge, skills, and values that are valued in the real world. Some researchers believe that developing some transferable people skills as well as technical skills is vital to pastoral ministry. Such skills include managing self, interpersonal communication, managing people and tasks, mobilizing for innovation and change, applied problem solving, vision casting, teamwork, and time management.

PART II

Pastoral Ministry
And
Leadership
Development

Chapter Four

Leadership Styles in the Church

We can fairly identify transformational leadership, servant leadership, spiritual leadership, leader-member exchange, transactional leadership, and laissez-faire leadership paradigms as leadership styles practiced in the church setting. Some of these models may be seen more frequently than others. In fact, over the last two decades, researchers and practitioners have become increasingly interested in the transactional and transformational leadership paradigms. According to Jens Rowold of the University of Muenster in Germany who has extensively studied pastoral psychology, several studies have been conducted to explore the effect of transactional and transformational leadership of pastors on several outcome criteria. Only a few, however, have tested the validity of this approach to leadership concerning Evangelical pastors. It is fair to advance that church leaders across many denominations appear to be transformational, servant leaders, spiritual, dyadic, transactional, and even laissez-faire leaders. In our study of SBC pastors' burnout, the aforementioned leadership styles were evaluated with respect to burnout and leadership development. We put a special emphasis on examining the transformational, transactional, and laissez-faire leadership paradigms to investigate which one is more prone to pastoral burnout.

Transformational Leadership

As its name implies, transformational leadership is a process that changes and transforms people. The transformational leader is a likable individual with a charismatic personality. Transformational leaders have the best interest of their followers in mind. They focus their attention on a vision which addresses the needs and values of the followers. They support, motivate, empower, and mobilize followers for a common goal. Transformational leadership occurs when one or more persons engage with others in such a way that leaders and followers raise one another to higher levels of motivation and morality. It is a relationship wherein leaders and followers raise one another to higher levels of motivation. Transformational leadership consists of four leadership factors including charismatic or idealized influence, inspirational, intellectual stimulation, and individualized consideration. Leaders, however, can be transformational or pseudo-transformational. There is a fine line between transformational and pseudo-transformational leaders. Leaders are truly transformational when they increase awareness of what is right, good, important, and beautiful; when they help to elevate followers' needs for achievement and self-actualization; when they foster in followers higher moral maturity; and when they move followers to go beyond their self-interests for the good of their group, organization, or society. Like the transformational leaders, pseudo-transformational leaders may also motivate and transform their followers, but they do it with a different agenda. They stimulate their support from followers for their own special interests and seek their own good rather than what's good for the group. They foster psychodynamic identification, projection, fantasy, and rationalization as substitutes for achievement and actualization. Peudo-transformational leadership can create a situational and amoral organizational atmosphere, which leads to chaos and even dissolution. It is prevalent in almost every aspect of the business world, and its impact on the organizations is enormous. Organizations, churches, and other businesses would be healthier and more productive if leaders and followers alike assume that anyone can be a leader. The practice of transformational leadership style is very important in the in the 21st century.

It can help leaders lead better as they face the leadership and organizational challenges in the new millennium. In the late 1990s and the early 2000s, a number of corruption scandals flooded the business community. Many top executives were accused of betraying the trust of shareholders. Pseudo-transformational leadership not only impacts organizations in a big way, but also has great effect on the morals of the society. In order to be truly transformational, leadership must be grounded in moral foundations. Researchers Bass and Steidlmeier asserted, "There are four components of authentic transformational leadership including idealized influence, inspirational motivation, intellectual stimulation, and individualized consideration". These components, they added, are contrasted with pseudo-transformational leadership on the basis of the moral character of the leaders, the ethical values embedded in the leaders' vision, articulation, and program; and the morality of the processes of social ethical choices and action in which the leaders and followers engage and collectively pursue.

Recent research shows correlations between the transformational leadership style and pastoral leadership effectiveness. In 2009, JC Carter conducted a study on pastoral leadership effectiveness. The results indicated that transformational leadership style showed significant correlations with pastoral leadership effectiveness. Seemingly, transformational leadership is helpful to pastoral ministry since it can help pastors avoid burnout. Burnout is found most often among those in helping or people related professions, among those who bear heavy responsibilities— therefore often among pastors. Pastors often face crisis throughout their ministry, which lead to stress and burnout. In order to help mitigate the effect of burnout, the minister must be a transformational leader. The transformational leadership styles help because when leaders are going through a crisis, they need trust and friendly relationships. Such trust can be created by charisma and inspiration. Transformational leaders are better equipped to handle crises, uncertainty, and threats that organizational changes and life circumstances create. Transformational leaders, throughout their endeavors, show endurance in mental, physical, and spiritual strength that truly inspire others to accomplish great tasks. But, pastors are not always transformational leaders. Some ministers embrace too many responsibilities. As a result they become stressed, frustrated, burned out and leave. In today's church community, congregants demand more out of their pastors than ever before. The minister must be well-equipped to serve the church community. It is not enough to just be a faithful preacher of the word. The tasks at hand are too great for one person to handle.

Thus, the minister must develop leaders. The clergy is responsible for spiritual guidance and development, motivation, restoration, care, correction, protection, unity, and encouragement of the followers. In many small and mid-sized churches, the pastor is responsible for the organizational development of the church and oversees the management of daily operations. The true transformer and effective pastoral leader is the one who develops leaders within the church body in addition to preaching, counseling, and worshiping. Unfortunately, some pastors equate effectiveness with being a good preacher and oftentimes they are unprepared to deal with administrative challenges.

Transactional Leadership

According to Burns, transactional leadership is a process which emphasizes the transactions or exchanges that take place between leaders and their followers. These exchanges are based on the leader's identification of performance requirements and clarification of the conditions and rewards that are available for meeting those requirements. There are three known dimensions of transactional leadership. These three dimensions are contingent reward—the degree to which the leader sets up constructive transactions or exchanges with followers: The leader clarifies expectations and establishes the rewards for meeting these expectations; active management by exception—the degree to which the leader takes corrective action on the basis of results of leader–follower transactions; and passive management by exception— the degree to which the leader waits until the follower's behavior has created problems before taking action. The difference between the three dimensions of transactional leadership resides in the timing of the transactional leader's intervention. Active leaders monitor followers' behavior, anticipate problems, and take corrective actions before the behavior creates serious difficulties. Passive leaders wait until the behavior has created problems before taking action.

Transactional and transformational leadership differ sharply. While transformational leadership is a process in which leaders offer a purpose that transcends short-term goals and focuses on higher order intrinsic needs; transactional leadership, in contrast, focus on the proper exchange of resources. The difference between transformational and transactional leadership is in terms of what leaders and followers offer one another. Transactional leaders do not individualize the needs of subordinates or focus on their personal development while the transformational leaders do. Transactional leaders are influential because it is in the best interest of subordinates to do what the leader wants since they receive incentives from him or her.

Servant Leadership

The model of servant leadership states that the leader's focus is on others rather than self and on understanding the role of the leader as servant. The term servant leadership was coined by Greenleaf in 1977. Since then, it has been used and advanced by many other leadership scholars. Greenleaf argued that by definition, servant leaders are to be servants first. It is the proven record of service offered by the leader that provides the basis by which the followers choose those who they want to follow. According to Greenleaf leadership is granted to those who are proven and trusted as servants. Servant leadership emphasizes the leader's role as steward of the resources including human, time, spiritual, financial, and physical in a church or organization.

Servant leaders have a great sense of humility. It is humility that describes what servant leadership should be. However, the modern-day leaders' rhetoric of love when dealing with followers often inspires more cynicism than genuine affection in those who do not understand the virtue of humility. Genuine love, which is a good quality of a person, produces humility. David Hume, in a work first published anonymously in 1739, noted that "the good qualities of others, from the first point of view, produce love; from the second, humility; and from the third, respect; which is a mixture of these two passions". Humility is a spiritual virtue. From a Biblical perspective, the Spirit of God gives grace to the servant leader. The Bible says: "God resists the proud, but gives grace to the humble" (James 4:6, New King James Bible, 1982).

The servant leader provides leadership in ways that encourage followers to become leaders in their own right and make decisions without regard to self-interest. Great leaders are humble individuals. Effective leadership behavior affects individual service quality; it also enhances team service quality. In a study conducted by Rude in 2003, he examined the rationale for a correlation investigation of servant leadership and burnout. Rude argued that servant leadership can play a substantial and pivotal role in reducing burnout in individuals.

Spiritual Leadership

The spiritual leadership style is defined by L.W. Fry as a style that comprises the values, attitudes, and behaviors that are necessary to intrinsically motivate oneself and others so that they have a sense of spiritual survival through calling and membership. Spirituality has been recognized as the essence of a person and as an essential part of an individual's wellbeing. According to Researchers Mitroff and Denton spirituality affects people's values, transcendence, the connection with self, knowing oneself and others. They argued that spirituality is the ultimate source and provider of meaning and purpose in people's lives.

Based on recent research findings, there have been increased interests in the positive effects of spiritual leadership in the practice of social work, especially on clinical and social practices during the past fifteen years. Spiritual people believe that leadership is an honorable ambition. Relationship building is one of the greatest strengths of spiritual leadership. J. Oswald Sanders said, "Warm relationships among team members are vital. Some workers prefer to administer; others want to love people. Only the latter are leaders". The spiritual dimension of an organization is its most fundamental source of power – its soul. Spiritual leadership identifies with something greater than the organization's bottom line. It identifies with the community or team and knows the greater good, which ultimately is best for the organization as a whole. Personal integrity, trust, authenticity are spiritual leadership's great strengths. When leaders display equitable, fair and unbiased processing of self-relevant information, personal integrity, and an authentic relational orientation, the relationship between the leader and the follower will be characterized by high levels of respect, positive effect, and trust.

While the vertical dyad relationship strengthens the interaction between leader and follower, a high level of trust and authentic leadership characterizes the relationship between the spiritual leaders and their followers. Spiritual leaders such as pastors and ministry leaders are highly esteemed by their followers. The belief is that leadership, from a Christian perspective, is a divine calling. As Kenneth Gangel stipulates, "Biblical leadership comes by divine appointment. It moves from singular to multiple and requires definitive accountability". Spiritual leadership requires credibility. One of the biggest challenges in leadership efforts is the credibility of the leader to get people to believe their message. As J.P. Kotter explained, many things contribute to credibility: the track record of the person delivering the message, the content of the message itself, the communicator's reputation for integrity and trustworthiness, and the consistency between words and deeds. Spiritual leaders have the best interest of their followers and organization in mind. They focus their attention on a vision which addresses the needs and values of the followers as well as the benefits of the organization as a whole. They support, motivate, empower, exercise unselfish love, empathize with followers, and mobilize them for a common goal. Moreover, spiritual leaders demonstrate their commitment through leadership by example. Otherwise the leader will be viewed as lacking integrity, unethical, and deceptive by the followers. Broken trust relationships between leaders and followers will make the vision difficult to sell and the mission accomplishment virtually impossible, which can negatively impact the organization. Leaders transform groups in ethically and morally uplifting ways. Spiritual transformation occurs when one or more persons engage with others in such a way that leaders and followers raise one another to higher levels of motivation and morality.

Researchers on several fronts raised the issue that it is necessary to establish the validity of spiritual leadership theory before it should be widely applied as a model to foster systematic leadership change on organizational and professional development levels. Many researchers such as Fry, Vitucci, and Cedillo called for more study to test the proposition that spiritual leadership theory offers promise as a catalyst for a new paradigm for leadership research and practice. They asserted that spiritual leadership incorporates and extends transformational and charismatic theories as well as ethics and values based theories such as authentic and servant leadership.

Furthermore, not all pastors are true spiritual leaders. Many of them are burned out, in part, because they are spiritually drained out. Based on a study conducted by Fuller Institute of Church Growth in 1991, eighty percent (80%) of pastors spend less than fifteen minutes a day in prayer, seventy percent (70%) say the only time they spend studying the Word of God is when they are preparing their sermon. As Christians, we believe that prayer and Bible reading make one a better spiritual leader. God works in individuals through the Holy Spirit to effectually bring about their salvation without cooperation from them. The spirit of God, however, with the cooperation of the leader, can help in the matter of pastoral burnout. God through the work of His spirit can remove anxiety, worry, insecurity, and guilt. G.L. Pinion stated that "one pastor admitted to have had a mental breakdown, because of stress, burnout, sin, and ignorance of God's direction in his life". He argued that the nature of depression in pastors is difficult to identify and treat. Pastors are often depressed before they realized it, unable to admit, or unaware of the shadows of depression haunting their lives and destroying their ministry.

While being spiritually led may help pastors avoid burnout, the problem may also come from their congregants, because not all church congregants are spiritually led. The reality is that many pastors are raging an internal battle with their own followers. According to Pinion, persecution of church leaders, in the North American context, does not come from outside the church. He asserted, "I have never had a pastor say to me, I am quitting. The pagans are getting to me! I have had more than I care to remember say, I can't take the Christians in the church anymore. I have had it with ministry!" The pastor oftentimes works under unhealthy conditions and hostile environments created by not so spiritual church members. Such environments cause them to be stressed out, frustrated and ultimately leave the ministry. Recent studies showed an enormous loss of pastors in the United States. The dropout rate is incredible. According to a report presented at the annual meeting of the Fellowship of Evangelical Seminary Presidents (FESP) in 2003, "pastors in the United States are dropping like flies". Pinion added that the report indicates "on the average, across the country and across all denominations, 1800 ministers leave the ministry every month".

Leader-Member Exchange (LMX)

Leader-Member Exchange style addresses the dyadic relationship between leaders and their subordinates, or members of their organizations. This is a style, which takes another approach of leadership and conceptualizes it as a process that is centered on the interactions between the leader and the followers. This theory suggests that leaders develop different relationships with each member of their organization, with the perceived quality of each relationship varying. As leaders develop relationships with their members, they form a group of members with high-quality exchanges loaded with a social support system called "in-group". The members who experience low-quality leader-exchanges with less social support are termed "out-group". According to P.G. Northouse, this theory works in two ways: it describes and it prescribes leadership. In both instances, the central concept is the dyadic relationship that a leader forms with each of his or her subordinates. Those who practice the leader-member exchange know how important it is to recognize the existence of in-groups and out-groups within a group or an organization. The relationships between in-group and out-group categories are not the same. In the in-group, the relationships are characterized by mutual trust, respect, linking, and reciprocal influence whereas in the out-group relationships are marked by formal communication based on job description. When the leader works with an in-group, it allows him or her to accomplish more, and the follower is willing to do more. Such relationship creates a communication flow between leader and follower to the benefit of the organization. The leader-member theory makes the leader-member relationship the pivotal concept in the leadership process.

The leader-member exchange is achieved through communication processes. Good communication is an essential skill to pastoral ministry. Every pastor should thrive to communicate effectively with members. A lack of communication between leader and follower may lead to burnout. Based on a research conducted by Becker, Halbesleben, and O'Hair in 2005, the relationship between defensive communication and burnout is mediated by perceived quality of leader-member exchange. The quality of the relationship between members and leaders should be related to the nature of their communication. Moreover, the relationship between members and leaders can reduce or aggravate burnout. There seems to be a correlation between leader-member exchange and burnout. Studies conducted on the relationship between leaders and followers and burnout within psychiatric rehabilitation workers indicated that the scores obtained from the leader-member exchange are significantly and negatively correlated with burnout scores.

An effective leader-member relationship creates a good work environment for both the leader and follower. Organizations are successful because they have good leaders and followers. Bad followers' behavior will eventually affect leadership behavior and effectiveness. Effective leader-member relationship enhances members' satisfaction and reduces burnout and turnover.

Pastors and church members have a leader-member relationship that interacts in two realms: physical and spiritual. Many biblical scholars are trichotomists, that is, they believe humans are three-part beings: body, soul, and spirit. Through his body, his soul lives and interacts in a physical world, and through his spirit, his soul interacts with the spiritual world. The LMX focuses directly on the relationship between the leader and the follower, which makes it similar to the spiritual leadership theory because it agrees with the stance that leader and individual followers can have unique relationships. The purpose of such relationships is the achievement of the leader's vision. Furthermore, pastoral ministry falls into the spiritual leadership category. Although these two theories have evolved over a different period of time, they are still being researched and used today to explain leadership styles and leaders' behavior. Spiritual leadership is a new way of thinking that views the leader as a whole. It views the leader in his/her four dimensional being, which consists of the body, mind (logical/rational thought), heart (emotions, feelings), and spirit (means of communication with God). It is assumed that a systematic application of the leader-member theory in pastoral ministry would improve pastor-congregant relationship, which ultimately would improve ministry satisfaction and reduce turnovers within the church.

Laissez-Faire Leadership

Laissez-faire leadership is the avoidance or absence of leadership. The earliest study on laissez-faire leadership was conducted by Lewin, Lippit, and White in 1939, a study which also included the democratic and authoritarian leadership styles. The laissez-faire leadership describes passive leaders unable or reluctant to influence or direct followers. Laissez-faire leaders avoid participating in group or individual decision making. Many researchers have argued that laissez-faire leadership style represents the absence of any leadership, transformational or transactional, thus it should be treated differently. Laissez-faire involves minimal leadership. The followers are left to work and perform their tasks with little or no interaction with the leader. As opposed to transactional leadership, laissez-faire represents a non-transactional style of leadership. Hence, laissez-faire is a non-leadership component and can be labeled as ineffective. However, some studies have demonstrated that the laissez-faire leadership style is not always ineffective, because in some cases, it can enhance the followers' performance. According to a study conducted by Bass in 1960, he contended that, in laissez-faire leadership, sometimes the autonomy of followers enhances their performance. But for the purpose of this study on pastoral burnout, the laissez-faire leadership style was briefly analyzed along with transformational and transactional leadership styles of pastors to explore the perceived pastoral burnout within the Southern Baptist Convention.

The Leadership Styles Compared

Transformational-transactional leadership, servant leadership, and spiritual leadership appear to have conceptual similarities. These styles make valuable contributions to the understanding of leadership. Although transformational, transactional, and servant leadership are more popular among researchers, spiritual leadership is somewhat similar to both. Spiritual leadership comprises values, attitudes, and behaviors necessary to intrinsically motivate one's self and others. The leader-member theory (LMX) and transformational theory have some similarities. The Leader-Member Exchange (LMX) is positively related to transformational leadership. Some transformational leadership factors predict the leader-member exchange. For instance, transformational leaders through charisma motivate followers to follow their lead through relationship building; while in the leader-member exchange, the followers strengthen and encourage the leader. The charisma of the transformational leader and individualized consideration of the LMX—both of which have been considered dyad-level influences that cause subordinates to behave in ways that strengthen relational ties with the leader.

There are similarities between servant leadership and transformational leadership concepts. The transformational leader's focus is directed toward the organization, and his or her behavior builds follower commitment toward organizational objectives, while the servant leader's focus is on the followers, and the achievement of organizational objectives is a subordinate outcome. Servant leadership is, at its core, a transformational approach to life and work, which has the potential for creating positive change in both leader and follower. Servant leaders seek to transform their followers to become servants like themselves. Furthermore, the aspiration that transformational leaders have to inspire others is also found in servant leaders.

The laissez-faire leadership style is very different from transformational-transactional, servant leadership, spiritual, and leader-member exchange. It is a leadership style in which leaders do not lead at all. In contrast to the aforementioned styles, the laissez-faire leadership style gives no feedback and provides little or no supervision. This leadership behavior eventually leads to job dissatisfactions, uncontrollable costs, bad service, failure, and a considerable rate of turnover.

Pastoral stress and burnout is a battle raging within many ministry leaders of the twenty-first century. There are, presumably, a number of leadership styles that many pastors practice in pastoral ministry. Since the early 1900s, there have been numerous leadership theories and studies presented. Historically, few studies have been conducted with respect to the leadership styles and their application to pastoral ministry. Pastors are placed in positions with high demands and expectations. They often play multiple ministry roles. Most pastors work long hours, often sacrifice time with family to tend congregational crises, carry long-term debt from the cost of seminary and receive below-average compensation in return for performing a difficult job. Trained in theology, they are expected to master leadership, politics, finance, management, psychology, and conflict management. Unlike other professions in which the leader provides help to others, such as doctors, psychologist, and so forth, they do not receive help in return. Thus, pastors are at great risk for burnout. This study attempted to determine the factors of pastoral burnout among pastors within the Florida Baptist Convention and evaluated the influence of leadership styles on pastoral burnout.

Chapter Five

Pastoral Leadership Competencies

Pastoral ministry of the 21st century needs capable leaders who know the Scripture well, able to teach, and lead the flock with competence. As leaders, pastors should be able to wisely apply their theological training to real life circumstances. Unfortunately, this isn't always the case. Over the years, many denominations have seen pastors move from one church to another, wounding congregations as they go. This is, in part, due to leadership incompetence. Let's be clear that no human is really competent enough to hold ministerial office in God's eyes. We can always find faults with pastors. As the apostle Paul asked the Corinthians, "And who is sufficient for these things?" (2 Corinthians 2:16, New King James Bible, 1982). Spiritually, pastors are not sufficient for the task given to them. They never have been. They will never be. They must rely on God to do the task He has given them. But, since they are dealing with humans, pastors need to be prepared to face the challenges inherent to their functions. The human problem is too big, human nature is too disabled, and human beings are perverse. So, pastors need to be ready for the requirements for pastoral ministry in the 21st century. We can't be "all things to all people", but we can at least prepare ourselves to face the challenges by learning the leadership competencies skills. Leadership is learned behavior, and the skills that make an effective leader are learned. Leadership skills are the ability to use one's knowledge and competencies to accomplish a set of goals or objectives. These skills including technical, human, and conceptual can be acquired and leaders can be trained to develop them.

Emotional intelligence

The concept of emotional intelligence (EI) was first applied to the business world by Daniel Goleman, an American psychologist who helped make the idea popular in 1995. He asserted that "truly effective leaders are distinguished by a high degree of emotional intelligence, which includes self-awareness, self-regulation, motivation, empathy, and social skill". Emotional intelligence (EI) is the ability to understand and manage both your own emotions, and those of the people around you.

Emotional Intelligence is one part of man's intellect. God gave man mental intelligence, the IQ that helps him to learn things, relational intelligence, which helps us to relate with others, and emotional intelligence. Emotional intelligence is perhaps the most intelligence we can have as human beings. It allows us to connect with people, and connecting with people can lead to success. Leaders who have emotional intelligence have the ability to feel a situation. He not only hears what's being said, and sees what's being done, but he feels the context of what's being said and what he has observed. People with emotional intelligence are connected with themselves first and then with others. This is what Goleman called self-awareness. Being self-aware when you're in a leadership position also means having a clear picture of your strengths and weaknesses.

Problem solving

Problem solving is used in a variety of fields for finding solutions to specific problems. In engineering, for instance, when a product or process fails, corrective action is taken to prevent further failures. Techniques such as Failure Mode Effects Analysis are used to proactively reduce the likelihood of problems occurring. In psychology, they define problem solving as the concluding part of a larger problem that also includes problem finding and problem shaping. The nature of human problem solving processes and methods has been studied by psychologists for more than two centuries. Human problem solving is driven by human emotions. Since pastors lead people, they have to understand the role of emotions in problem solving. So, when approaching a problematic situation involving people, pastors need to understand that problem solving consists of two related processes: problem orientation, which is the motivational, attitudinal, affective approach to the situation, and the problem-solving skills. In some cases, pastors may have to refer to experts or even to government authorities for more complicated matters.

Problem solving is part of the conflict management process; and that is inevitable when dealing with people. Conflict will always occur when two or more social entities disagree on the recognition and solution to a task problem, including differences in viewpoints, ideas, and opinions.

There are many approaches to problem solving, depending on the nature of the problem and the people involved in the problem. Some approaches to problem solving include the description and clarifying of the problem, an analysis of the causes, identifying the alternatives, assessing each alternative, implementing the chosen alternative, and evaluating whether the problem was solved or not. One major problem that leaders face when making decisions is a lack of experience and knowledge. One way to make sound and informed decisions is to have the knowledge of the field one is in. Knowledge is power and the decision making process comes with some level of power. Good decisions cannot be made if the leader is working under considerable unmanaged stress. Usually, stress arises when an individual perceives the environment as demanding because it exceeds his or her resources and threatens personal well-being. Stress should be managed if one wants to be effective in the pastoral ministry. Inadequate staffing is also another hindrance to pastoral leadership. It is stressful to work when staffing levels are inadequate. In order to be effective, church leaders must have competent and reliable staff, which should help to alleviate their task and their contribution to the success of the church.

Vision casting

A vision is a picture of the future seen in the present. To every man God called, a vision is given. The greatest gift a man could ever receive from God is to be able to see his future from the present. A pastor's vision is a picture of what God wants to do. Whatever the vision may be, communicating and casting it are incredibly important to the visionary. Pastors are visionaries who see their future in faith. Church congregants often need direction and the opportunity to see before they believe and embrace a vision.

A fisherman in order to catch fish has to cast his line into the sea far enough to attract them. The same is true for the leader. The visionary pastor has to cast his vision of the future far and wide in such a way as to attract, train, and retain his followers who will see his vision to completion. Vision Casting, means making your idea of your church, ministry, or project known. And it works best when you cast your vision in a way that motivates, inspires, and encourages your followers. Those followers you need to catch the vision and really believe in it. Sometimes we have a vision, but our followers can hardly tell what it is. It is our job to make it known.

Mobilizing for innovation and change

Change is always occurring in organizations, churches, and businesses. A change can be a good thing, but is more beneficial when we are prepared for it. Usually, an organization can benefit more from change it is prepared for versus change that is imposed on it. As we prepare for change, we also need to learn how to identify the need to change and to manage it successfully. This learning capability will allow us to address future problems and take advantage of opportunities more quickly. The ability to embrace change is essential to success in any profession. Pastors who want to lead effectively in the 21st century must embrace innovation and change. Innovation inherently requires some level of change. Change requires learning. People tend to learn when something new happens. People react to events. So, change always triggers something that will motivate the followers in new learning. And it can come from both internal and external sources. For instance, new technology, leadership and personnel change, etc.

Leadership change is a big issue in many churches when a pastor leaves. Sometimes people go astray and followers are hurt due to the sudden departure of a leader. Effective leaders help followers to accept and embrace change in their environment so that when change occurs, its impacts on them may be minimal and therefore avoid distractions or dispersion.

Time management

Time is something leaders and followers alike have an equal amount of. Time management is defined as a process of planning and exercising control over the amount of time one has to spend on specific project or activities to increase effectiveness, efficiency or productivity. Time management include planning, allocating, setting goals, delegation, analysis of time spent, monitoring, organizing, scheduling, and prioritizing. So, leaders should never "kill time". Time management, in reality, is self-management. The leader has to manage the self rather than the time. We get 24 hours of it and that's all. So we don't really manage time.

The best use of time is not to manage it. The best use of time is to manage oneself. So, in time management, basically, what we need to do as leaders is to take the time we have and do what we need to do. If we do that correctly, then time becomes our friend or a good co-laborer rather than something we fight or someone we run against. But if we use our time incorrectly, then it becomes something we bear with and kill until the next important project comes. The challenge we may have is to log the time. Once time is logged, it is controlled and we may say that we have managed ourselves well and used our time correctly. If we manage ourselves well, we have control over what we do in time. It's a leader's choice when it comes to time management.

Learning to Communicate Effectively

Any leadership that leaves out the ability to communicate effectively is doomed to fail. Communication skills however often start with the ability to be open and receptive to the attitudes, ideas and opinions of others. It is also the ability to empathize and understand a person's circumstances. These are fundamental building blocks that should be put in place to reduce the probability of conflicts, misunderstandings and low performance.

Pastors need to listen to God's voice as well as their followers. Through prayer, a pastor can constantly and effectively communicate with God. As a leader, the pastor needs to communicate effectively with his followers. If a leader is isolated from what is going on around them they'll have shut themselves down to the flow of vital information about what is going on in the organization. Apart from simply being aware of the day to day operations it is imperative to be able to listen to what is "not" being said, meaning the general mood state of one's followers and/or peers. The mood state can significantly affect, even undermine the optimism, enthusiasm and morale of the people. Keeping a finger on the pulse of this subtle but important piece of information will help the effective leader to know well in advance when the wind is about to blow in the opposite direction. This will help them take swift corrective action before it's too late.

Learning to be Confident

Self-doubt is readily perceived by the church members and can, not only undermine their confidence in you as the pastor, but it can also spread like a wild fire through the church leading to loss of focus, enthusiasm, and trust in the overall mission of the church. The ability to trust one's self, can be perceived as exhibiting an internal, unwavering, confident steadiness that inspires confidence and optimism in followers.

Learning to Empower Others

With power comes a feeling of responsibility that often makes some pastors feel like they must do everything themselves. Unfortunately this often overwhelms them and under powers the church administration. It also neglects the valuable resources and strengths that exist in the powerful synergy of individuals working together as a high performance team. An effective leader knows and trusts the strengths of their followers and how to nurture self confidence in them so that they can fully express their creative potential. Empowerment includes encouraging, and developing peoples' skills, training, and educating followers. It is a pastor's responsibility to develop his followers to do the work that is expected of them so that they can contribute to the growth of the church and the people who serve it. Leaders who empower followers put their attention on people development and see them as their most valuable asset. Their leadership success, however, will depend on their ability to surround themselves with an inner core of competent people who compliment their leadership style and goals.

Learning to be Resilient

Resilience is defined as the ability to not let the negativity in. Competent leaders have the ability to deflect any and all stress from having an effect on them. They are aware of the stressors that can jeopardize their leadership functions and avoid them at all costs. This entails cultivating a state of inner emotional strength and vitality that can help them weather any storm. As the captain of the ship the competent pastor must be able to steer the church both in good and bad times effortlessly and confidently without wavering emotionally. That's the resilient pastor.

Learning to Take Responsibility

A good leader realizes that they have been charged with significant responsibility for the vitality of the organization and ultimately for the lives of the people that are a part of it. Too often the pastor's agenda takes precedence over the fact that the followers are the engine or life blood of the church. So, when the welfare of the church and the spiritual well-being of the people are neglected, that can severely cripple any agenda or programs a leader has. In this light a good leader recognizes their role and responsibility to those who work in the church and exhibits an unwavering concern for them.

PART III

Leading Factors
Of
Pastoral Burnout

Chapter Six

Factors Leading To Pastoral Burnout

Based on the participants in the study, the following factors were evident to influence pastoral burnout. First, one-third (33.3%) of the participants felt that dealing with people while trying to help them to become better Christians was a substantial challenge that could lead to pastoral burnout. Twenty-five percent (25%) said working too hard is a contributing factor in pastoral burnout. Twenty-five percent (25%) cited that Staff issues, time management problems, and money-raising requirements, were also common factors that could lead to pastoral burnout.

Half of the participants (50.0%) were not satisfied. One participant stated "I do not feel I'm near as effective" while another stated that "I'm very dissatisfied . . . I see so many unfulfilled goals and objectives that I haven't yet achieved."

Forty-one percent (41.7%) said they were satisfied with their effectiveness, and some (16.7%) were satisfied but still driven to improve their pastoral performance. Based on the responses, it appears that dissatisfaction with their personal effectiveness as a pastor may be an issue related to job performance, great achievement, and spiritual fulfillment. Dissatisfaction with one's performance could lead to burnout. Therefore, job performance, apparently, is among the factors contributing to the SBC pastoral burnout and ministry turnover.

Furthermore, fifty percent (50%) of pastors felt that their workload was light; another fifty percent (50%) felt that their workload was heavy. Nearly all of the participants felt that serving in their current position had not negatively affected their health, which is a key symptom of burnout. Despite the fact that the participants did not appear to be extensively burned out, a considerable number of them indicated substantial levels of work-related stress. One-third of the participants felt that burnout was associated with pastoral turnover. Many pastors described burned out pastors as pastors who lost their love for the people.

Although some pastors described a burned out pastor as depressed or having lost their love for people, physical and emotional tiredness were more common descriptions. Pastors were asked to provide evidence that serious symptoms associated with burnout were alleviated with a strong support system. Nearly all of them indicated that they had such a system.

Apparently, many pastors who participated in the study were able to combat the potential negative effects of burnout in a variety of ways. They understood that a high-quality staff that was properly managed was important to prevent pastoral resignations. Despite the fact that half of the pastors were not currently satisfied with their effectiveness, this did not appear to cause undue stress, as many of them showed some reticence to refer to oneself as effective, possibly driven by a desire to improve their performance regardless of their current level of effectiveness. They understood that surrounding oneself with a high-quality staff was important to making the work manageable. One pastor stated that "Now I have a good church to work with and really good lay leaders. Just amazing, some of them have seminary degrees . . . so that sort of makes my job easier. This is probably one of the most giving, most hard working, and sacrificial church I have been in a while".

We created a burnout inventory in which we asked more than one hundred pastors to indicate how frequently they faced some type of crisis that required their attention. More than nine percent (9.4%) of them indicated that they faced such a crisis daily, 34.4% faced such a crisis more than once a week, 12.5% faced such a crisis once a week, and 43.8% faced such a crisis less than once per week. When they were asked to state their level of agreement to the statement "I think leadership training might help me to overcome some of the job related problems", 15.6% of them strongly agreed with this statement, 53.1% agreed. Only 12.5% of the participants strongly disagreed with this statement while 6.3% disagreed. A total of 12.5% of the pastors neither agreed nor disagreed with this statement.

We also asked them, "How do pastors' leadership styles relate to pastoral burnout?" Their responses indicated that pastors who were more inclined to exhibit transactional leadership, particularly the contingent reward version of transactional leadership, tended to have lower overall levels of burnout. Pastors who were more inclined to practice laissez-faire leadership tended to have higher levels of burnout. Thus, pastors' leadership styles do play a role in pastoral burnout. Specifically, pastors who exhibited a transactional leadership style tended to have lower levels of burnout, while pastors who exhibited a laissez-faire leadership style tended to have higher levels of burnout.

When attempting to group the pastors based on their dominant leadership style, it was determined that 96.9% of the pastors exhibited primarily a transformational leadership style, with only 3.1% exhibiting a transactional leadership style, and none of the pastors exhibited a laissez-faire leadership style.

In order to allow for some comparison between pastors' leadership styles and burnout, and given the dominance of transformational leadership styles, we made a comparison among individuals with varying preferred forms of transformational leadership. Twenty-five percent (25.0%) exhibited primarily an inspirational motivation form of transformational leadership, eighteen percent (18.8%) exhibited an individualized consideration form of transformational leadership, fifteen percent (15.6%) exhibited primarily an idealized influence—behavior form of transformational leadership, three percent (3.1%) exhibited primarily an idealized influence—attributed form of transformational leadership and another (3.1%) of pastors exhibited primarily an intellectual stimulation form of transformational leadership. The remaining pastors did not exhibit a preference for any of the five forms of transformational leadership. Based on these frequencies, we created four groups: 1) those who exhibited an inspirational motivation form of transformational leadership; 2) those who exhibited an individualized consideration form of transformational leadership; 3) and those who exhibited an idealized influence—behavior form of transformational leadership; and 4) all others (34.4%). These results indicated that the type of transformational leadership the SBC pastors exhibited was not significantly related to their levels of burnout.

Most of the pastors who participated in the study did not feel that they were extensively burned out. Burnout was typically manifested with being tired as opposed to more serious symptoms such as depression or a desire to leave the ministry. The pastors were able to combat the potential negative effects of burnout in a variety of ways including having a high-quality staff and knowing how to manage their staff. Pastors who were more inclined to exhibit transactional leadership, particularly the contingent reward version of transactional leadership, tended to have lower levels of burnout. Those who were more inclined to practice laissez-faire leadership tended to have higher levels of burnout. The practice of transformational leadership was not significantly associated with levels of burnout.

Although too few pastors had strong transactional or laissez-faire leadership styles to perform the planned comparisons of leadership style and burnout, supplemental analyses indicated that the specific type of transformational leadership did not significantly relate to burnout levels.

There is evidence in previous studies by other researchers that pastors are at risk for burnout, because not enough study exists on the topic and its impact on the functions of the pastor and few studies have explored the effects of leadership development theories on pastoral burnout. Thus, less research has been devoted to understanding leadership development as it is related to pastoral burnout. We utilized two different methodologies to gather data from pastors. We interviewed them and conducted a survey. The different sources of data were used in order to identify perceived pastoral tress, burnout and differences in outcomes between pastors' leadership styles. These were revealed in both the surveys and interviews.

Several directions for further study of additional factors impacting pastoral burnout and ministry turnover among pastors in the Southern Baptist Convention are apparent from the findings. So, we recommend that further studies to be conducted, which may include the role of pastors' wives in ministry. Often pastors' wives function in less "pastoral roles" in the SBC than do their spouses. This study lacks responses of pastors' wives and their perceptions on pastoral burnout.

The level of stress a minister is experiencing with respect to levels of support received may be significant in its impact on him. Since most studies on burnout show stress as a contributing factor, further research examining a pastor's level of stress and support system and the relationship to burnout would be helpful. This study could have been enhanced by adding a measure of the pastors' level of stress. Perhaps, a Likert scale in which each pastor would rate his current level of stress from a scale of 0 to 10 in the current burnout inventory maybe helpful.

Another area that warrants further research is the impact of specific denominational factors on pastoral burnout. The role a denominational system plays in one's ministry may be a significant influence on burnout. Each denomination functions under its own rules and traditions that may foster or reduce pastoral burnout.

Future research should also include multiple states studies and educational level of participants for the additional comparison of demographic and economic factors and a larger mix of pastors. Such research should also include extended studies that focus on the perceived benefits of leadership development of startup churches' pastors. We would also recommend that further research be conducted on ministry turnover as it relates to job satisfaction and personal accomplishment.

Chapter Seven

The Future of Pastoral Leadership

The most significant finding regarding this study was that factors of leadership competencies such as emotional intelligence and feelings of personal accomplishment have a significant relationship to pastoral burnout. It is noted that pastors who stated that dealing with people and staff issues as their greatest challenges have also expressed some dissatisfaction and some feelings of personal accomplishment. Those with greater work and life experience who have developed greater leadership competencies and resources that foster greater feelings of personal accomplishment have been able to minimize the feelings of emotional exhaustion. Thus, the quality of social support was highly significant for emotional exhaustion.

What is most significant is that pastors who practice transformational and transactional leadership styles have lower levels of burnout. Pastors, who throughout their endeavors, show endurance in mental, physical, and spiritual strength that inspire their followers while setting up constructive transactions and exchange with them experience less burnout.

There is an urgent need for training in social sciences and leadership competencies with an emphasis on leadership styles to minimize pastoral burnout. This would create opportunities to increase awareness of pastoral burnout in denominations around the world and begin an informed future of pastoral ministry through effective training and mentorship that have implications for ministers entering the ministry.

Formal support system should be a priority for pastors who wish to have a successful pastoral career that would positively impact their ministry. The Southern Baptist Convention's church planting program and other denominations should include formal training in burnout prevention, emotional intelligence, and leadership styles as part of their church planting curriculum. The self-rating tools used in this study may become part of an ongoing process of comparing data and pastors' comments to improve job satisfaction and minimize ministry turnover. The development of a pastoral mentoring program could be a useful tool assisting church planters who are less experienced pastors.

Taking Action
Action Steps to avoiding Your Burnout

You can prevent your burnout

Be aware of potential problems. The best way to be aware of these problems is to listen to the people close to you. During your ministry, always maintain a consistent devotional life. Sometimes, we ask others to do it while we neglect ours. Let's lead by example. Accept your limitations—you can't be all things to all people. Use your common sense. Some things you do or decisions you make will affect your family. Think about how they may affect your family, physically, mentally, financially and spiritually.

Furthermore, you need to balance what is most important in your life and seek out and enjoy the simple things in life. Take time off and vacations often. Learn to forgive others when you're disappointed. Create a support system for yourself—have at least one person you can talk to with problems. I would encourage you not use a member of your church as a person you talk to when you have ministry problems. Have an accountability partner, a mentor or someone who has more experience than you to help you when you are facing the ministry challenges.

Since you know your strengths and weaknesses, do the ministry you are gifted and called to do. Put your family before your ministry. Nurture your family before you nurture the church. If you feel stressed out, take care of it by getting the help you need. If you don't manage your stress it may lead to burnout and the later may lead to depression. It is difficult to identify and treat depression in pastors, because they are often depressed before they realized it. Many of them are unaware of the shadows of depression that is haunting their lives and ultimately destroying their ministry.

Pastors beware! In real estate, there is a term called caveat emptor used regarding the closing date of a property. Generally, caveat emptor is the property law principle that controls the sale of real property after the date of closing. Basically, it means let the buyer beware! So, to prevent pastoral burnout, my brethren, beware! Let the pastor beware!

PART IV

Self-Help Tools

Stress and Burnout Inventory

The following questionnaire may be used to evaluate one's level of stress and burnout.

1. I face some type of crisis that requires my attention on a

   _____daily basis
   _____more than once a week
   _____once a week
   _____2-3 times each month
   _____ more than 3 times a month

2. The crises I face contribute to burnout

   o Strongly disagree
   o Disagree
   o Neither agree nor disagree
   o Agree
   o Strongly agree

3. The responsibilities I have contribute to burnout

- o Strongly disagree
- o Disagree
- o Neither agree nor disagree
- o Agree
- o Strongly agree

4. Sometimes I feel I can't take it anymore.

- o Strongly disagree
- o Disagree
- o Neither agree nor disagree
- o Agree
- o Strongly agree

5. Sometimes I feel like quitting my profession

- o Strongly disagree
- o Disagree
- o Neither agree nor disagree
- o Agree
- o Strongly agree

6. Sometimes I feel the stress of my profession is more than it should be

   o Strongly disagree
   o Disagree
   o Neither agree nor disagree
   o Agree
   o Strongly agree

7. I receive good support in dealing with job related problems from church members

   o Strongly disagree
   o Disagree
   o Neither agree nor disagree
   o Agree
   o Strongly agree

8. Sometimes I feel like I don't know how to lead the church

   o Strongly disagree
   o Disagree
   o Neither agree nor disagree
   o Agree
   o Strongly agree

9. I feel like I am going to burn out

   o Strongly disagree
   o Disagree
   o Neither agree nor disagree
   o Agree
   o Strongly agree

10. I feel like I have already burned out

   o Strongly disagree
   o Disagree
   o Neither agree nor disagree
   o Agree
   o Strongly agree

11. On a scale of 1-10 with 10 being burned out, how would you rate your degree of burnout?

   ___1-3
   ___4-6
   ___7-8
   ___9-10

12. I think leadership training might help me to overcome some of the job related problems

- ○ Strongly disagree
- ○ Disagree
- ○ Neither agree nor disagree
- ○ Agree
- ○ Strongly agree

My Leadership Growth Goals

Leaders do not grow by chance. It must be intentional. Leadership growth requires a plan. Here you can add any goals that you may have for your personal growth.

Goal#1:_____

Goal#2:_____

Goal#3:_____

Goal#4:_____

Goal#5:_____

Your goals are your individual work plan for your leadership growth. This exercise will be helpful through your entire leadership journey. Your individual goals represent the areas of leadership you want to improve.

A Plan for Personal Growth

"No leader can lead someone to a place where he or she has not been" (John C. Maxwell)

Paul's instructions to Timothy regarding personal growth (I Timothy 4:13-16)

It takes personal efforts to grow.

Gifts without growth = ineffectiveness

1) Growth is essential for you as a leader (v. 16)

2) Growth is essential for those you serve (v. 16)

3) Growth benefit both you and those you serve (v. 15)

Seven Steps to Personal Growth

1) Start with yourself

2) Get rid of excuses

3) Take no short cuts

4) Be positive and hopeful

5) Make an effort to grow every day

6) Be mindful of what is necessary and essential

7) Make a personal decision to change

A Word to Pastors of Central Florida and Around the World

The ability to lead the flock of God is the greatest privilege ever given to man. Serving as a pastor is a remarkable and awesome blessing and honor. You get to equip the saints of God for eternity. What office is higher and has greater significance than that of a pastor? You were born to be a pastor. God may have taken different pathways, perhaps long and awkward ways before you get to this point. But you were born again to be where you are. This pastoral gift was given to you by God almighty. He knows how to work it for His glory. As you know, a pastor is one of the five office gifts the Lord gave to the church. Paul said to the Ephesians, "And He Himself gave some to be apostles, some prophets, some evangelists, and some pastors and teachers, for the equipping of the saints for the work of ministry, for the edifying of the body of Christ, till we all come to the unity of the faith and of the knowledge of the Son of God, to a perfect man, to the measure of the stature of the fullness of Christ" (Ephesians 4:12-13, the New King James Bible, 1982). So, pastoring is a gift and you happen to be a gift that God gives to a church.

You didn't become a pastor by accident. This is part of God's purpose and plan for your life. The purpose of a man is the reason for his existence. God has a plan for every man's life before he was even born. In fact, this plan had been in place before the foundation of the world. It is this plan that unfolds in the word of God. From eternity past God's desire has been to make Himself known, and all creation is His way of doing that. It is through you that His ultimate plan is to be realized. God had something in His mind when He gave you the gift of pastor. It was to equip, edify, and nurture His people, the flock until we all come to the unity of the faith and of the knowledge of the Son of God. Let me remind you that dealing with people is difficult. President Theodore Roosevelt once said, "The most important single ingredient in the formula of success is knowing how to get along with people". Being a pastor requires that you work closely with people. What makes people difficult is that they can be unpredictable, different, and have different needs, which often change. They also desire and respond to different leadership styles, and are gifted with different strengths, skills, and talents. That's why you need to learn to lead the flock from both sides of the leadership equation, the human side and the spiritual side. Remember, man is threefold: body, soul, and spirit. If we are in the business of guarding souls, we have to be mindful of all three parts of man while leading the flock. The reason is, as you know, God created man in His own image and likeness. He is expressed and represented through man. In order for this to happen, He created each part of man with a specific function in relation to His purpose and plan. The problems pastors face in the church are also tripartite. Some are emotionally, physically, or spiritually driven. We have to go to the source in order to understand the driver and pinpoint the underlying root cause. That's why pastors must be emotionally intelligent. Monitor your own feelings and that of your followers and peers. Be aware of your own strengths and weaknesses. We all have our strengths and weaknesses. The apostle Paul went through a lot of crisis throughout his ministry, but he held on. He was shipwrecked, stoned, beaten and laughed at, but he kept going. His strength in weakness is a model for all pastors who go through periods of crisis. He bore a great deal of scars on his body for the Lord. Let no one cause me trouble, Paul wrote to the Galatians, "for I bear on my body the marks of the Lord Jesus" (Galatians 6:17, King James Bible, 1982). As Charles Swindoll noted, Paul's marks signified his sufferings for Christ . . . and every one of those scars was a permanent reminder that he belonged to his Master, Jesus. You belong to God and He sees your marks, visible or invisible. Your marks may not be seen by your followers and peers, but they are clearly seen through the eyes of the Spirit of God.

Pastoring is truly the highest privilege. But sometimes pastors can be the most misunderstood people in the church. Often their hours are longer than others in the workforce, their pay is minimal, the criticisms they receive are considerable and constant. Despite the joys of serving God, feelings of disappointment and discouragement can plague their lives to the point of quitting the ministry. Just remember, pastoring is not a job. It is a gift. You can be fired from a job, but nobody can take away your gift. Your gift is eternal.

May this book ignite the passion of purpose in the heart of every person called to serve God in a very special and unique way. May you be inspired to pursue and fulfill the vision He has put in your heart. Leaders don't quit. They may have made mistakes, but they keep moving. May the Lord Jesus, who called you to His work, give you the help you need as you keep moving forward.

Bibliography

Asgari, A., Silong, A.D., Ahmad, A., & Sama, B.A. (2008). The relationship between transformational leadership behaviors, leader-member exchange and organizational citizenship behaviors. *European Journal of Social Sciences, 6*(4), 140-151.

Baggi, S. (2008). *Pastor Pain: My Journey in Burnout.* Palm Beach, Queensland, Australia: Actuate Consulting.

Barna, G. (2006). *Pastors feel confident in ministry, but many struggle in their interaction with others,* http://www.barna.org/barna-update/article/17-leadership/150-pastors-feel-confident-in-ministry-but-many-struggle-in-their-interaction-with-others; accessed *November 6, 2009.*

Bass, B.M., & Steidlmeier, P. (1999). Ethics, character, and authentic transformational leadership behavior. *The Leadership Quarterly, 10*(2), 181-217.

Baucum, C.L. (2008). A Study on Intrinsic Motivational Needs and Engagement of Leaders. Capella University: Minneapolis, MN.

Becker, J.A., Halbesleben, J.B., & O'Hair, H.D. (2005). Defensive communication and burnout in the workplace: the mediating role of leader-member exchange. *Communication Research Reports, 22* (2), 143-150.

Burns, J. M. (1978). *Leadership.* New York, NY: Harper & Row.

Carter, J.C. (2009). Transformational leadership and pastoral leader effectiveness. *Pastoral Psychology, 58,* 261–271.

Fry, L.W. (2003). Toward a theory of spiritual leadership. *The Leadership Quarterly 14,* 693–727. Retrieved November 29, 2008 from http://www.regent.edu/acad/ sls/publications/conference_proceedings/servant_ leadership_roundtable/2005/pdf/parolini_invest.pdf.

Gangel, K.O. (1997). *Team Leadership In Christian Ministry.* Chicago, Ill: Moody Press.

Goleman, D. (1996). *Emotional Intelligence. Why it can matter more than IQ.* London: Bloomsbury Paperbacks.

Greenleaf, R. K. (1991) *Servant leadership: A journey into the nature of legitimate power and greatness.* New York, NY: Paulist.

Hawkins, O.S. (2003). *High calling, high anxiety: Advice from James for managing stress in ministry.* Dallas, TX: *Annuity Board of the Southern Baptist Convention.*

Hume, D. (1739). *A treatise of human nature.* Retrieved from June 10, 2009 http://ebooks.adelaide.edu.au/h/hume/david/h92t/B3.3.6.html.

Jayaratne, S. & Chess, W. (1984). *Job satisfaction, burnout, and turnover: A national study.* Washington, DC: *National Association of Social Workers.*

Jin, Y.S. (2009). *A study of pastoral burnout among Korean-American pastors.* (Doctoral dissertation, Liberty Theological Seminary, 2009). *University Microfilm International, 3352424.*

Klaas, A.C. & Klaas, C.D. (1999). *Clergy shortage supply.* Mithville, MO: *The Lutheran Church.*

Kotter, J.P. (2001). What leaders really Do. *Harvard Business Review, 68*(3), 85-96.

Lombardo, M. M., & Eichinger, R. W. (2000). High potentials as high learners. *Human Resource Management, 39,* 321-329.

Malphurs, A. (2003). *Being leaders: The nature of authentic Christian leadership.* Grand Rapids, MI: Baker.

Maslach, C., & Leiter, M. P. (1997). *The truth about burnout: How organizations cause personal stress and what to do about it.* San Francisco, CA: Jossey-Bass.

McArthur, J. (1995). *Rediscovering pastoral ministry.* Dallas, TX: Word.

Mitroff, I. & Denton, E.A. (1999). *A spiritual audit of corporate America: A hard look at spirituality, religion, and values in the workplace.* San Francisco, CA: Jossey-Bass.

Murphy, R. A. (2002). *Statistics about pastors.* Retrieved March 5, 2009 from http://www.maranathalife.com/lifeline/stats.htm.

Niebuhr, H. R. (1956). *The Purpose of the Church and Its Ministry.* New York, NY: Harper and Brothers.

Northouse, P.G. (2004). *Leadership: Theory and practice.* Thousand Oaks, CA: Sage.

Pinion, G.L. (2008). *Crushed: The perilous side of ministry.* Springfield, MO: Twenty-First Century.

Rassieur, C.L. (1984). *Stress management for ministers.* Philadelphia, PA: The Westminster.

Rowold, J. (2008). Effects of transactional and transformational leadership of pastors. *Journal of Pastoral Psychology, 56* (5), 403-411.

Sanders, J.O. (1994). *Spiritual Leadership.* Chicago, Ill: Moody Press.

Swindoll, C. (2009). *Paul: A Man of Grit and Grace.* Nashville, TN: W. Publishing Books.

Warren, R. (2006). *God's answers to life's difficult questions.* Grand Rapids, MI: Zondervan.

http://hirr.hartsem.edu/research/fastfacts/fast_facts.html

About The Author

W. Ruben Exantus, Ph.D.

is an international educator and leadership consultant. He is known as a leader in organization and management and conducts research in leadership, strategic management, and ethics. He is founder and pastor of Grace Baptist Church in Orlando, FL and also the founder and managing director of Rex Institute for Research and Leadership Development. Most of Exantus' work has been devoted to providing nurture and guidance to Christians, whether young or old in the faith; they have become over the years the center of his ministerial work.

He constantly writes on leadership issues and Bible study guides, which give practical help to many of the people who attend his study sessions. He has studied at Northeastern University of Boston, Massachusetts, Gordon-Conwell theological seminary, Luther Rice Theological Seminary, and Capella University where he obtained advanced degrees in engineering, theology, and organization and management with a specialty in leadership respectively. Exantus is a scholar in the field of spiritual leadership with certifications in clinical pastoral education (CPE). He lives with his family in the northwest of Orlando, Florida.